Winding Ways Quilts

A Practically Pinless Approach

Nancy Elliott MacDonald

Publisher:
Amy Marson

Editorial Director:
Gailen Runge

Editor: Pamela Mostek

Technical Editor:
Franki Kohler

Copyeditor/Proofreader:
Stacy Chamness

Cover Designer:
Kristy Konitzer

Book Designer:
Nancy Biltcliff

Design Director:
Diane Pedersen

Illustrator:
Kirstie McCormick

Production Assistant:
Matt Allen

Photography:
Sharon Risedorph

Published by:
C&T Publishing, Inc.
P.O. Box 1456
Lafayette, California
 94549

Front cover:
Flower Garden Ways

Back cover:
Fiesta! and *Purples Galore*

Attention Copy Shops: Please note the following exception—Publisher and author give permission to photocopy pages 71, 72, and 73 for personal use only.

Attention Teachers: C&T Publishing, Inc. encourages you to use this book as a text for teaching. Contact us at 800-284-1114 or www.ctpub.com for more information about the C&T Teachers Program.

We take great care to ensure that the information included in this book is accurate and presented in good faith, but no warranty is provided nor results guaranteed. Having no control over the choices of materials or procedures used, neither the author nor C&T Publishing, Inc. shall have any liability to any person or entity with respect to any loss or damage caused directly or indirectly by the information contained in this book. For your convenience, we post an up-to-date listing of corrections on our web page (www.ctpub.com). If a correction is not already noted, please contact our customer service department at ctinfo@ctpub.com or at P.O. Box 1456, Lafayette, California, 94549.

Trademarked (™) and Registered Trademark (®) names are used throughout this book. Rather than use the symbols with every occurrence of a trademark and registered trademark name, we are using the names only in the editorial fashion and to the benefit of the owner, with no intention of infringement.

Cataloging-in-Publication Data
MacDonald, Nancy Elliott.
  Winding ways quilts : a practically pinless approach / Nancy Elliott MacDonald.
    p. cm.
  ISBN 1-57120-234-X (Paper trade)
  1. Patchwork—Patterns. 2. Machine quilting—Patterns. I. Title.
  TT835.M264 2004
  746.46'041—dc22

                        2003022034

Printed in China
10 9 8 7 6 5 4 3 2 1

Dedication

To Grace and Charlie Elliott, my parents. They brought me up to do the best I could at whatever I decided to do.

To Ann Elliott Stuart and Judy Elliott Spivey, my big sisters. They tell me I'm wonderful just about no matter what I do!

To my sons, Will and Dan, my grandchildren, Desmond and Hannah; and my stepkids, Katie and Rob and their families. They're always surprised by what Mom/Grandma/Nancy's been up to lately.

The quilters whom I may never meet, but whose future quilting experiences may be enriched by something they learn from this book.

And, most of all, to Colin "Mac" MacDonald, my husband, partner, friend, cook, advisor, mistake finder, super copy-machine operator, and devil's advocate. He makes me laugh and keeps me on track.

Thank you all.

Acknowledgments

Many people have had a part in making it possible for me to write this book: My thanks to all of them, and especially to:

Darra Williamson, then-editor-in-chief at C&T, who thought I had a book to write. Pamela Mostek, my editor, who helped me coax the book onto paper. Franki Kohler, my technical editor, who made my instructions work, and the entire staff at C&T for putting it all together.

Mrs. Bill's Lakers - Helen, Jaime, Kitty, Elizabeth, and Patty, who encouraged my quilting from day one and are my patient guinea pigs for new techniques and workshops.

The many quilting teachers, authors and colleagues who taught me much of what I know about quilting and gave me the confidence to develop my own techniques.

The River City Quilter's Guild, which has been my quilting anchor since the beginning.

My students, who often teach me more than I have taught them.

Thank you one and all.

Table of Contents

Introduction

Welcome to my curvy world.

I'm Nancy Elliott MacDonald, and I like to call myself a curvy lady! I'm so glad you're reading this book to learn about curved piecing by machine. After learning about my easy technique, I'll bet you'll soon be a curvy person yourself!

First a little about my background. My introduction to quilting was purely "hack and slash"—meaning strip piecing and straight lines, squares and rectangles. Before long, I noticed a quilt pattern that looked something like a cloverleaf and formed circles when the blocks were joined together. Quilts made from this pattern, which was called Winding Ways or Wheels of Mystery, appeared periodically in various quilting magazines.

I was drawn to that pattern while still in horror of the dreaded curved seam, the also dreaded "T" word (*templates*, of course), and the even more dreaded hand piecing concept. In 1992, I finally bit the bullet, made some templates, drew around them on some fabric I didn't like, and hand pieced a few. Placed on my design wall, the circles did, indeed, appear. I was hooked. The love affair had begun.

Pulling lots more fabrics I didn't like very much, I pushed ahead. The line drawing, pinning, and hand piecing were a real pain in the neck, but the circles kept coming on the wall and they were so neat. I soon moved to the sewing machine and gradually used fewer and fewer pins and no seam clipping until I developed the system you'll learn in this book—one pin. (Actually two are needed on the last seam—surely you can allow me that little exaggeration.)

It was because of this pattern that I began my teaching and lecturing career and now, wonder of wonders, here is my first book. By the way, that first Winding Ways quilt was named *Uglies* (page 62) after those fabrics I didn't like. Actually, it is one of my favorite quilts. Maybe I need to rethink my color preferences.

I tell my students that they shouldn't worry about the perfect design or the perfect fabrics or perfect points . . . or anything else that is perfect in their quilts. What they should worry about is getting that top done and finishing it into a quilt. Make your choices, finish the quilt, and get busy on the next one. Every quilt you finish prepares you to do a better job on the next one and the one after that. Perfect comes with practice. A finished quilt is always my goal.

At the time of writing this book, I've made at least 40 Winding Ways quilts. They are kind of like my sons' descriptions of skiing days—some are better than others, but none are bad, and a few are really incredible. An unlimited number of variations are possible through the use and placement of different colors, patterns, values, and block sizes. It's safe to say that we'll never finish exploring the possibilities because every time I teach Winding Ways, a student comes up with a new twist. In fact, in *Art Quilt Magazine* several years ago, I saw that quilt artist Marilyn Pikey had even portrayed human figures with this pattern. How about that!

One curved pattern led to another as I developed more patterns and classes. To make life easier for my students, I've developed my own templates for these other curved designs, as well as for Winding Ways. For purchase information, see Resources on page 79.

Now, please join me in this adventure of sewing curved-seam quilt patterns. Once you master Winding Ways, you'll be able to sew just about any curved-seam pattern like a pro. I can hardly wait until you send me photos of *your* Winding Ways quilts!

nancymac

Winding Ways— My Way!

BEFORE YOU SEW

Your love affair with Winding Ways is about to begin. Before we get to the fun part, the sewing, there are a few things to learn. Don't panic—it won't be difficult, and once you learn them, you're on your way. When I'm teaching this technique, I get lots of sighs and groans from my classes when we start. Soon, however, they become so excited about the possibilities that they charge through the essential information, devouring it as quickly as possible so that they can sew blocks. I know you're excited to get to that part, too, so let's get started on your Winding Ways adventure!

Fabrics, Fibers, and Batting

Don't worry if you find fabric selection to be a daunting task. Many quilters worry about whether their fabric choices are "good." I have a rule about this subject. If YOU love the fabric, then it is a "good" choice. There might be a better choice for value or graphic impact, but if you don't love what you're working with, it won't be fun doing the work.

So just relax about choosing your fabrics. It's better to enjoy making the quilt and learn how to make the next one better, than to spend a week worrying about whether you made the right fabric choice.

Even though there's lots of room for choices when selecting your fabrics, one thing to keep in mind is their value. In Winding Ways quilts, value is extremely important. In this section you will find specific tips for choosing the light and dark fabrics for your Winding Ways quilt.

If you can't decide on two fabrics, go directly to one of the variations using lots of fabrics. The more different fabrics you use, the less important each one becomes. When in doubt, instead of pondering over which blue to choose, use 12 different blues of a similar value.

I prefer to use high-quality, 100% cotton fabrics. Bargains abound in some fabric stores but the quality of the fabric may be questionable. Many of these bargains are what I call "starched cheesecloth"—when you wash them there's nothing left. High-quality fabrics, such as those found in quilt shops and well-known mail-order and Internet stores, will last for many, many years. To paraphrase that well-known slogan: "You're worth it!" Please don't cut corners on the fabric. Harriet Hargrave's book, *From Fiber to Fabric*, explains all of the fine points of fibers and fabric.

Prewash or Not?

I prefer to prewash everything I can. That way, I figure I'm covered for any possible shrinkage and bleeding colors. When I bring the fabric home, I zigzag the cut edges and wash it on the gentle cycle with a little Orvus™ paste, which I use for washing all my fabric and quilts. It is available in most quilt shops.

 I LIKE TO HAVE everything together when I start a quilt. If you don't work this way, put the backing, sleeve, binding, and batting where you'll be able to find it later when the finishing urge strikes.

Some of my good friends never wash a fabric. I tell them, "It only takes one bleeding fabric to ruin a quilt!"

If all goes well with the washing and drying procedure, I generally just fold the fabric and put it away. If it comes out wrinkled, of course I press it carefully with my steam iron. Occasionally I find I need to press fabric when I later pull it from the shelves to use it.

Batting

Before I use a batting, I check the labels and instructions to see if it can be prewashed. Since I prewash all my fabrics, I like knowing I've prewashed the batting too! If it can be washed, I wash it. I soak the batting in warm water for about 10 minutes, then spin out the water and dry in the dryer on "low" or "air." Always follow the manufacturer's directions carefully or you may end up with a washer full of loose fibers that will be useful only for stuffing toys! Some of my good friends never wash a batting before using it. It's a matter of personal choice.

I recommend cotton or mostly-cotton batting for machine quilting. It helps to keep the layers from slipping. There are many choices now for cotton batting. Check them out in your local quilt shop or through Internet or mail-order sources.

Some hand quilters prefer to use Polyester batting because it's so easy to quilt through. That's okay for them, but my advice is to stick with cotton batting if you're quilting by machine. For more information on batting, again check out *From Fiber to Fabric*.

Fabrics for Winding Ways Quilts

To make sure that the circles in the Winding Ways design pop out, here are a few tips to keep in mind when you're selecting your fabrics. As a general rule, you'll get the most dramatic results if you choose fabrics with high value contrast.

--Fabric 1---

We'll call this your Dark, but it can actually be medium-dark to dark. For value, multi color prints work well, and bright and intense colors are also good. This fabric should definitely be something you love because it sets the mood or theme of your quilt. I start with a multi-color print because they are designed by artists who know what they are doing with color. Use the knowledge of those professionals. Looking carefully at a multi color print fabric gives clues about value, complements, and proportions of color. Be careful of prints with large areas of both dark and light values. They will make finding the right Fabric 2 very difficult.

--Fabric 2---

This is your Light fabric. When you place it next to your Fabric 1 (Dark) it should have strong contrast in value as well as color with little or no obvious pattern. For Fabric 2, use a fabric with a different color and value from Fabric 1. It's easy to lose the circles in the design when the fabrics are too closely matched.

--Fabric 3---

I often add a narrow container border next to the pieced area to stop the action and add a bit of "zing" to the quilt. Sometimes I use a real Zinger fabric, being careful it's not too overpowering. Fabric 1 usually offers a clue to help you find the right Zinger. I look for the color used the least in the print fabric. In saturated form, it can be very effective as a Zinger. This saturated form is simply a more deeply or richly colored version of a paler color in the print fabric. A Zinger is optional and sometimes excessive, depending on the other fabrics and border designs.

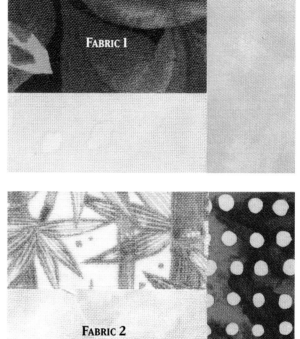

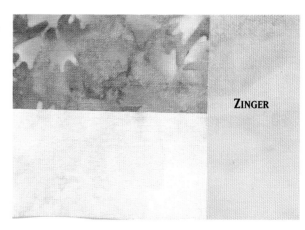

BLACK OR VERY DARK fabrics may be difficult to piece if lighting is less than wonderful. I have trouble piecing black even if the lighting is good! Of course, using black with almost any other color will usually give a striking design result.

Putting the Fabrics Together

In all of these examples, the blocks would be made from two fabrics. A Zinger border would be used, and the outer borders would be Fabric I. The fabric combinations you see here are examples of good choices that will result in a great Winding Ways quilt.

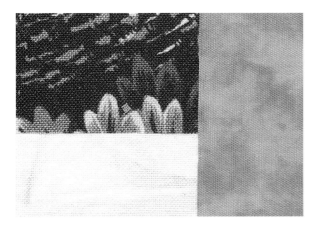

Remember, there are no bad fabrics. There are only fabrics that have been unsuccessfully combined with other fabrics. Strong value contrast between the fabrics will enhance the pattern.

You should love the fabrics you use. That's my first rule. After loving the main fabric, the others can be chosen to enhance it.

Check Them Out

For a final check of your fabric combination, try the squint test. Look at strips of the two fabrics with your eyes squinted almost shut. If each fabric stands on its own, they should work in the design. To help you determine color, you might try a Ruby Beholder, found at quilt shops, a clear, red plastic report cover from an office supply, or a reducing glass from an art supply store to help you determine value. My eyes do as good a job for me as any of the tools I've tried, but if there is a tool that will help you, by all means use it.

All About Templates

Now that you know everything there is to know about selecting your fabrics, it's time to move on to the next essential item—the templates. The best and easiest to use are commercially produced acrylic rotary-cutting templates. My own die-cut acrylic rotary-cutting templates are available for Winding Ways patterns and other curved designs. See Resources on page 79. Several vendors offer templates, sometimes known as Wheel of Mystery or Circles of Mystery, and these may be available in your local quilt shop or through Internet and mail-order sources.

Or perhaps you can persuade a friend with a motorized jigsaw or band saw to cut a set of templates from $1/8$" scrap acrylic sheets you can purchase inexpensively at a plastics store. Actually, I made my first several Winding Ways quilts using templates I made myself. When it looked like I would be making a lot of these quilts, I found someone to cut acrylic templates for me: first a friend in his workshop, then a professional who now produces all of my templates.

Making Your Own Templates

If you just can't wait and have to make your own, you may have materials on hand that will work. Two layers of template plastic can be glued together with rubber cement for a firmer template. A plastics shop should have remnants of material that can be cut with utility scissors or a craft knife. Linoleum-type material or even an asphalt or vinyl floor tile might work. And, there's always file folder cardstock. When using these homemade templates for rotary cutting, be very careful. As the edges become distorted with repeated use, they must be replaced. Directions follow to make your own templates.

 WHETHER YOU MAKE YOUR own templates or use purchased templates, accurately drawing the line, as shown on page 10, is an important step. If you use purchased templates, be sure to remove the protective paper covering before drawing the line. Sometimes I think this is the hardest part of the process!

TO MAKE YOUR OWN TEMPLATES, HERE'S WHAT YOU'LL NEED:

☐ *Tracing paper*

☐ *Permanent fine-line marking pen*

☐ *Paper-cutting scissors*

☐ *Rubber cement or glue-stick (I like rubber cement)*

☐ *Template or stencil plastic sheets*

OR

☐ *"Cut-able" vinyl or linoleum-type floor tile*

OR

☐ *File folder*

☐ *Utility scissors or utility knife or heavy-duty craft knife.*

For the Winding Ways block, you will need templates A, B, and C on pages 71-73 in whatever size you choose.

--STEP 1--Trace the template patterns carefully with a permanent pen onto tracing paper, leaving approximately ¹/₂" between shapes. With paper scissors, cut out the shapes, leaving about ¹/₄" outside the line.

--STEP 2--Glue the rough-cut shapes to template material. When dry, use utility scissors or knife to cut out the templates on the traced line. Be sure to protect your table surface if you are using a utility or craft knife.

--STEP 3--Refer to the template drawing below. With a ruler and a fine-line permanent marker, draw a line across the narrowest part of Template C, ¹/₄" from the end, or actually place the acrylic template on top of the paper template and trace on the line.

Non-skid Material

Adding non-skid material such as sandpaper dots or other material available for that purpose to the back of each template will make cutting much easier. Which side is the back? It doesn't matter—they're reversible so just choose one side. Here's an easy idea: I discovered if I brushed rubber cement on the back and let it dry well, the template would stay put.

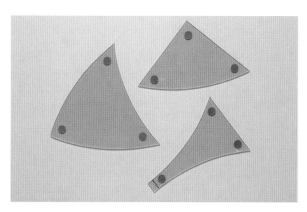

Preparing the Fabric

We're getting closer to actually sewing! But first I'm going to show you a cool way to cut out the Winding Ways pieces using a fabric rectangle with a tricky "magic" fold that makes putting the block together a smoother process. I love this technique and so do my students. It's practical for quilts with 2 fabrics or scrap quilts. Several of the projects require more selective value and fabric choices, which are addressed in the project instructions. For the others, this technique works great. So stay with me, follow the directions and here we go!

Fabric Rectangle with the Magic Fold

Before cutting the pieces for the blocks, a fabric rectangle must be cut to specific dimensions. Use the chart below to determine the cutting size of the fabric rectangle, then follow the steps.

Rectangle Cutting Chart

Finished size of block	Single Set	More than one set (Whole widths or scrap pieces)
3 inch	9½" × 5"	9½" × width of fabric
6 inch	15½" × 7½"	15½" × width of fabric
8 ½ inch	22" × 10"	22" × width of fabric
9 inch	22" × 10"	22" × width of fabric
12 inch	29" × 12½"	29" × width of fabric

--STEP 1--Cut a fabric rectangle of the required size.

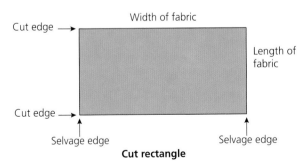

Cut rectangle

--STEP 2--Fold with wrong sides together, matching raw edges. The selvage edges will be at the ends. Place carefully on your ironing board and press the fold well.

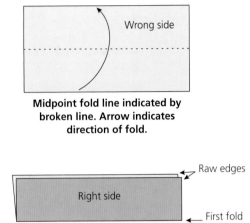

Midpoint fold line indicated by broken line. Arrow indicates direction of fold.

First fold complete

--STEP 3--Bring the folded edge up toward the raw edges, leaving a space approximately ³⁄₈" between the fold and the raw edges. If the raw edges aren't visible, stop and correct the fold. When fold is placed correctly, press the new fold well. The folded rectangle is now ready to use.

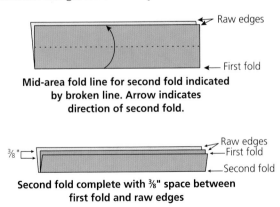

Mid-area fold line for second fold indicated by broken line. Arrow indicates direction of second fold.

Second fold complete with ³⁄₈" space between first fold and raw edges

Folding Smaller Rectangles

If you want to make a quilt using several fabrics you'll want to cut smaller rectangles of more fabrics. The chart on page 11 shows the minimum size fabric rectangle for the magic fold process. Use it to determine the size of the fabric rectangles you'll need to cut.

--**STEP 1**--Cut a fabric rectangle the size you need.

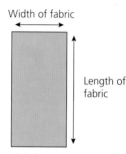

Width of fabric

Length of fabric

Cut fabric rectangle

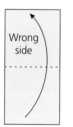

Wrong side

Midpoint fold line indicated by broken line

--**STEP 2**--Place the narrow ends together with the right side up. Press the fold.

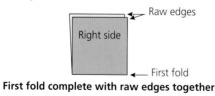

Raw edges

Right side

First fold

First fold complete with raw edges together

--**STEP 3**--Bring the folded edge up toward the raw edges, leaving a space approximately ³⁄₈" between the fold and the raw edges. If the raw edges aren't visible, stop and correct the fold. When fold is placed correctly, press the new fold well. The folded rectangle is now ready to use.

Right side

Mid area fold line for second fold indicated by broken line. Arrow indicates direction of right side.

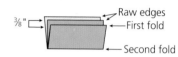

³⁄₈"

Raw edges
First fold

Second fold

Second fold complete
³⁄₈" space between first fold and raw edges

Using Strips Instead of Folded Rectangles

Several of the projects in the book require that the pattern pieces are cut from strips rather than from the folded rectangles as shown above. Each project includes cutting instructions for that particular variation. Strips are also practical for seriously scrappy quilts.

When using strips, you will cut C pieces exactly the size of the templates, without the fold. Then two of the C pieces must be sewn together at the narrow end. I have done this many times and it works fine—just not as slick as the other way.

 HERE'S A HANDY TIP for making Winding Ways quilts. Plan ahead so you'll know how many pieces to cut—half dark and half light. Try to be organized, keeping track of the pieces as you cut them. Write it down on a note pad, adding as you go, so you know when to stop. It's a real pain to have to stop sewing to cut more pieces. On the other hand, if you cut too many, there's the beginning of another quilt. And the quilt series begins!

Cutting the Pieces

Now that the fabric rectangles are cut and folded, it's finally time to cut out the pieces! All of the projects use these steps, so it may be helpful to refer back to this section as you work on the individual projects. Before we get started cutting, let's look at a few terms I will be using as we go through the steps.

I refer to the group of pieces that make each Winding Ways block as the set. A set includes four A pieces, four B pieces, two short C pieces, and one long C piece, which was cut on the fold for a total of four C pieces. The A pieces will be one value, and the B and C pieces will be the opposite value. The instructions for each project will tell you a specific number of sets of each value to cut.

When you sew this set of pieces together, it becomes the block, which is the basic unit that makes up each quilt. The sets of each value that you have cut will be rearranged and sewn together into positive and negative blocks.

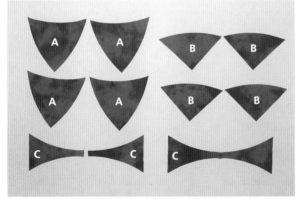

Cut set of dark fabric

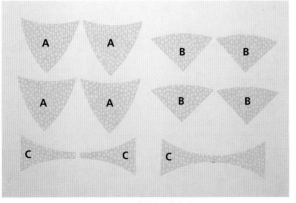

Cut set of light fabric

I LIKE TO USE a 28mm rotary cutter to cut curved pieces. It works better for me on the innie (concave) curves. Some of my students get along fine with the standard 45mm ones, which give me problems by nicking the blades on the acrylic templates when cutting the innie curve.

Cutting with the Folded Rectangle

Below you'll find the layout diagram for cutting the block pieces. This is as frugal a cutting arrangement as I've found, so I recommend using it for your Winding Ways blocks. It also helps to keep track of the number of pieces cut. Follow the steps below for placement and cutting of the pieces.

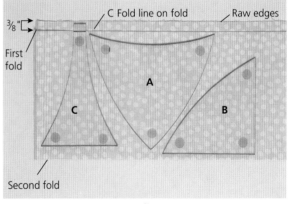

Layout diagram

--**Step 1**--Place the templates as closely together as possible while not cutting off any corner points.

--STEP 2--Place the C template with the $\frac{1}{4}$" line on the fold. The raw edges should be extending approximately $\frac{3}{8}$" beyond the fold and beyond the narrow end of the template. Cut out with 28mm rotary cutter.

--STEP 3--Slide Template A as close as possible to the first cut, cut out the A pieces. Slide Template B as close as possible to the last cut, cut out the B pieces.

--STEP 4--When you have completed the cutting in Steps 1–3 you will have one set of block pieces. Cutting in the same order—C, A, and then B—continue cutting across the folded rectangle until you've cut the required number of sets for your project.

--STEP 5--Once the required number of sets have been cut, rearrange them into new sets so that the Light A pieces are matched with the Dark B and C pieces, and the Dark A pieces are matched with the Light B and C pieces.

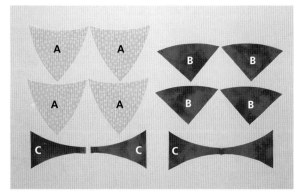

Pieces for Block 1

Pieces for Block 2

Cutting with Fabric Strips

For scrappy quilts or for most of the book projects—*Graphic Medallion, Pastel Medallion, Amish Stars, Fiesta!,* and *Medallion of Four*—fabric strips may be a more practical cutting strategy. The project instructions specify the number of strips to cut, the strip size, and the number of pieces to cut from each template.

When using strips, cut a series of the same shape, rotating the template to the best cutting advantage. It is helpful to keep track of the pieces as you cut them out. If you need only a few pieces of one fabric, cut only the widest fabric strip. Cut the larger templates first, then the smaller ones.

Using a Pair of Scissors

I encourage my students to use a rotary cutter to cut out their pieces. It may seem awkward at first, but you'll get better at it. Some quilters prefer to use scissors, and this folding technique will work with scissors. You just need to make a few adjustments.

To use the templates without a rotary cutter, follow the folding, layout and cutting instructions, except when folding the rectangle, place right sides together so that the wrong side will be outside. Place templates on wrong side of the folded rectangle or fabric strip, then trace around the templates with a pencil, permanent fine-line pen, or other marker that is visible on the fabric.

Pin each piece through the folded layers so that they don't shift. With the layers pinned together, cut the pieces out with good, sharp scissors. If you have trouble cutting layers of fabric, trace each shape as many times as is needed and cut the shapes out individually.

SEWING THE BLOCKS

I've taught this method to hundreds of students, some very experienced and others needing to be shown how to use a rotary cutter. So, if you are a beginner or if you just don't feel comfortable sewing curved seams, follow the steps carefully and practice. It will get easier.

The pieces in Winding Ways blocks have gentle curves. The seams are sewn with one, or at the most, two pins. The curves are not clipped with my technique. If you follow the directions and diagrams, you should be able to master my easy, easy method for machine-sewing curved seams. You'll want to read this section over several times. Then, cut out a few blocks and practice the techniques as you go. Once you catch on to the new and different way of handling your pieces, you should soon be on your way to practically pinless curved-seam machine sewing.

Just a note—this technique will not work as well on small, tight curves, such as small Drunkard's Path blocks. But, hey, once you know how easy the looser curves are to sew, why would you want to do small, tight curves!

Very Important Stuff

Tips

Before we begin sewing, here are a few tips to keep in mind. They may not all be clear as you read through them, but as you venture into the piecing process you will understand them. Once you get all this Very Important Stuff into your head, or at least know where to look back in this section to find it, piecing curved seams will be easy for you!

■ All of the curved seams in this book are sewn using the same technique. The shorter seams will require only one pin. The last seam in the block will require a second pin.

■ As you begin to sew the pieces together following the instructions and diagrams, you may feel like it's the first day with your new hands. Expect to be somewhat awkward until you have sewn a few blocks. Be patient and hang in there—it will come to you.

■ When pinning, take only a tiny "bite" of fabric right at the seam line. This bite of fabric has nothing to do with the snack you wish you were having right now. In this case the bite is how much fabric you pick up between where the pin goes IN and where the pin comes OUT. A tiny bite is maybe two or three threads, which allows you to maneuver the layers as they move under the presser foot toward the needle. A large bite won't let you do that.

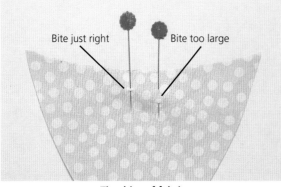

Tiny bite of fabric

■ The outer edges of both the concave and convex pieces measure differently, but the seam lengths are the same. Rather than pinning and clipping, you will be manipulating the pieces to keep the edges in line with each other. It's kind of like setting a sleeve into an armhole in dressmaking—only easier!

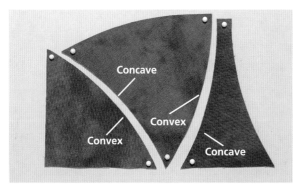

Concave and convex seam lines are the same.

■ Do not trim corner points. These are very helpful in matching pieces for accurate piecing. Stitch from edge to edge with $1/4$" seam throughout.

■ When using four C pieces, two of them must be sewn together on the narrow end before assembling the block. I recommend reducing the stitch length for this tiny seam.

■ You may occasionally need to stop, needle down, and lift the presser foot to help relax and adjust layers. Just lifting the foot will usually do the trick. Then replace the presser foot and continue sewing.

■ Different fabrics will behave differently. If both fabrics are the same quality weave, they will almost piece themselves. If one fabric is softer or finer or much heavier than the other, they will require more attention. Batiks and pima cottons will fight you some because they have such a dense weave. If you have problems of this type, just slow down and stop every few stitches (needle down) to adjust things. Slow stitching will prevent the dreaded UN-stitching.

■ You will need something pointy in one hand as you stitch. It must be sharp enough to grab the fabric layer. It could be a stiletto, seam ripper point, embroidery scissors point, large needle or pin, quill, awl or other pointy tool. I used a seam ripper for years but must confess that when I finally got a stiletto, it worked much better. The stiletto, or other pointy tool, is essential to help manipulate the fabric layers right under the needle.

Definitions

This is the last of the Very Important Stuff you need to know before starting to sew. These terms are the key to following and understanding the block construction directions. Look at the pieces and think about them as though you were sitting at the sewing machine getting ready to sew. In fact, going over this part at the sewing machine might be a really good idea.

Leading edge—This is the edge of the fabric that goes under the needle first. It is the edge that is away from you as you sit at your machine.

Following edge—This is the edge of the fabric that goes under the needle last. It is the edge nearest to you.

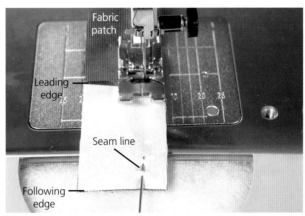

Leading and following edges

Innie—This is the concave curve on your Winding Ways pieces. Always place it on top of the outie when you start sewing your seam.

Outie—This is the convex curve on your pieces. It is the opposite of the innie curve.

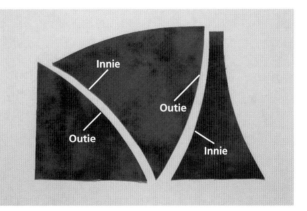

TO AVOID CHEWING UP the fabric at the beginning of a seam and having all those threads underneath, try the folded fabric patch. As you see in the photo above, fold a scrap of fabric in half that is about 2" × 2". Position it just before the seam you'll be sewing. Start the seam on this fabric piece, not the actual project, then stitch through the fabric piece right into the seam. Chain all the pieces with one of these at the beginning and the end of the chain. Remember, it's not about saving thread—it's about great piecing!

The Winding Ways Seam

At last it's time to sew! Before you begin, read through the steps below for sewing the curved Winding Ways seam, then carefully follow each step. Try a practice block before you start sewing the blocks you've cut for your project.

--**STEP 1**--Establish your 1/4" seam allowance on your machine. Double check to make sure it's accurate.

--**STEP 2**--Set your stitch size to a fairly small stitch, about 2.5 European or about ten stitches per inch. We're not planning on ripping out seams if we can help it, but, just in case, don't make the stitches too tiny!

--**STEP 3**--With the right sides up, lay out the pieces for one block next to your sewing machine.

--**STEP 4**--Choose the two pieces you are going to sew first. Lay the Innie piece back on top of the outie piece, right sides together.

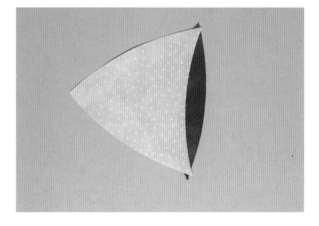

--**STEP 5**--Pin the following edges together with two tiny bites along the seamline.

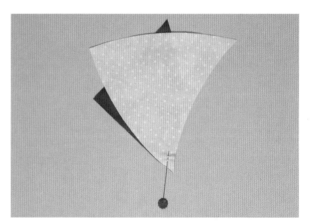

--**STEP 6**--Place the leading edges together, holding them in position with the thumb and forefinger of the left hand while starting them under the presser foot.

--**STEP 7**--Take two or three stitches and pause with the needle down in the fabric.

--**STEP 8**--With your left index finger against the pin, pull the fabric toward you to slightly stretch the two pieces.

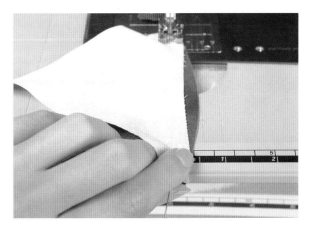

--**STEP 9**--Keeping the tension taut, place your left index finger halfway between the following pin and the needle and hold the two layers in place.

 IF YOU DON'T HAVE a quarter-inch foot, place a see-through ruler under the presser foot with the quarter-inch line under the needle and the ruler edge to the right. With the ruler square on the machine surface, lower the needle just until it touches the quarter-inch line. Lower the presser foot. Place several layers of masking tape right up against the edge of the ruler. You can also use 3 to 4 Post-It® note sheets with the sticky edge against the ruler.

--STEP 10--Holding the stiletto in your right hand, use it to pull piece A to the right. At the same time, place the middle finger of your left hand between the pieces, resting it on the lower piece and pulling it to the left if necessary. Sew a few stitches at a time, stopping with needle down, whenever you need to.

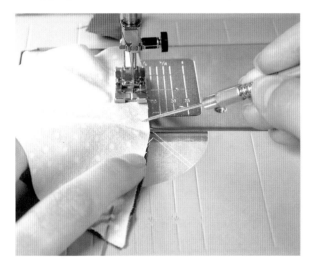

--STEP 11--Continue sewing until you approach the following end, taking a few stitches at a time and keeping the edges even. The top layer will try to pile up in front of the presser foot so keep track of it. Here's where your stiletto comes in handy! You can use it to urge the fabric under the presser foot as you go, or raise the presser foot as before and adjust the seam. Carefully pull the pin out as you get to the end of the seam, but leave it in as long as possible to keep the ends in shape.

 EVERY TIME YOU STOP (with needle down, of course), and get ready to stitch again, apply a little pressure by pulling against the pin to equally divide the seam area between the pin and the sewing machine needle. That's the little "stretch" move to set up your stiletto action again.

--Step 12--After you've sewn the seam, finger press, smoothing the seam toward the outie curve. The curve should be flat.

And you've done it! You've just mastered the key to machine piecing curved seams—my way! The reward for hanging in there is that your friends will think you are really clever and smart and such an incredibly talented piecer! Good for you! But, just in case you're not feeling really comfortable with the curved seam yet, you may want to make a few more seams with your practice blocks.

Now here's what I consider some very important advice. It takes a little concentration at first to master curved seams, so be sure your muscles aren't getting tense. Stop every 15–20 minutes. Sit up tall, shoulders back, head straight, chin tucked to chest, hands relaxed in your lap. Now squeeze your shoulders together, down and back for a few seconds, release and do it again several times. Then roll your head on your neck. Doesn't that feel good? Now get back to work!

 IF YOU THINK IT'S absolutely necessary, you can use an extra pin at the beginning of the seam. Be sure and place the pin out of the way of the presser foot. On longer seams, such as the 12" Winding Ways blocks, you may find it helpful to add a pin at the center point as well. Matching centers, pin with a tiny bite across the seamline.

Making the Winding Ways Block

Now that you've mastered the curved seam, it's time to use it to put together the Winding Ways block. You may find it helpful to read through the instructions before you begin sewing, and refer to The Winding Ways Seam section if you need to review.

First, sort the cut pieces into blocks so that you will have the pieces for one block. Let's start by making a Block 1, which has a dark background. You need 4 Light A pieces, 4 Dark B pieces, 2 Dark short C pieces, and 1 Dark long C piece.

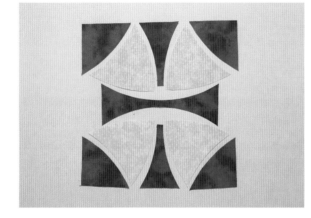

You will make Block 2 following the same steps, but you will reverse the positions of the light and dark pieces. Each project will tell you how many of Block 1 and Block 2 you will need to complete it. First, sew the pieces into units, and then sew the units together to complete the Winding Ways block.

Unit 1

--**STEP 1**--Place the 4 Dark B pieces and the 4 Light A pieces next to the sewing machine with right sides up. Referring to The Winding Ways Seam on page 18, sew the A pieces to the B pieces to make 4 of unit 1 for Block 1.

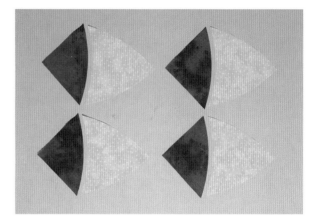

Unit 2

--**STEP 1**--Place 2 of unit 1 and 1 Dark short C piece next to the sewing machine with right sides up.

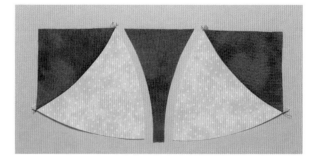

--STEP 2--Turn the Dark short C piece back on top of one unit 1 and pin the following edge as shown. Sew the seam, keeping the raw edges together and maintaining the 1/4" seam with fingers and stiletto.

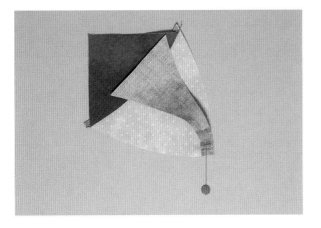

--STEP 3--Finger press the seam toward unit 1, keeping the narrow post of the Dark short C piece flat.

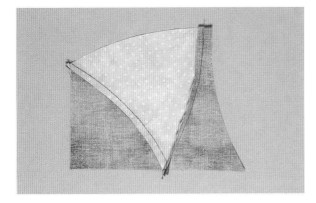

--STEP 4--Repeat Steps 1–3 using a second unit 1 and second Dark short C piece. You now have 2 of unit 2.

Unit 3

--STEP 1--Place 1 unit 2 and 1 unit 1 next to the sewing machine with right sides up as shown.

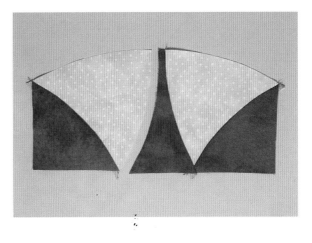

--STEP 2--Turn unit 2 back over unit 1 and pin the following edges as shown. Sew the seam, keeping the raw edges together and maintaining the 1/4" seam using your fingers and stiletto.

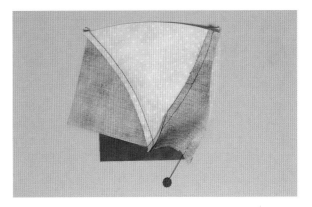

--STEP 3--Finger press the seam toward unit 1, keeping the narrow post of Dark short C flat.

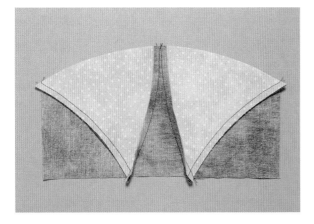

--STEP 4--Repeat Steps 1–3 using the second unit 2 and second unit 1. You now have 2 completed unit 3's.

Unit 4

--STEP 1--Place the 2 unit 3's and Dark long C piece next to the sewing machine with right sides up.

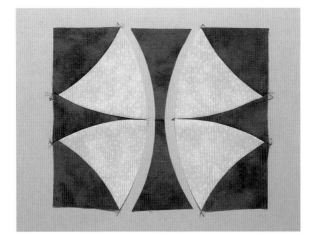

--STEP 2--Fold the Dark long C back over one unit 3 as shown. Match the center of the Dark long C piece to the seam in the middle of unit 3. Pin across the seamline at the centerline and along the seamline at the following edge.

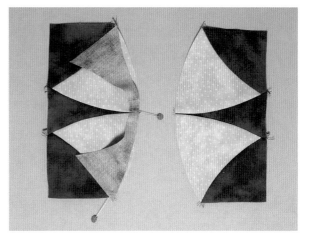

--STEP 3--Sew the seam, keeping the raw edges together and maintaining the $1/4$" seam with your fingers and stiletto.

--STEP 4--Finger press the Dark long C piece toward unit 3. You've now completed unit 4.

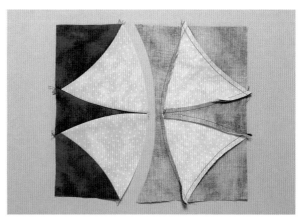

Completing the Block

--STEP 1--Place unit 4 and the second unit 3 next to the sewing machine with right sides up as shown.

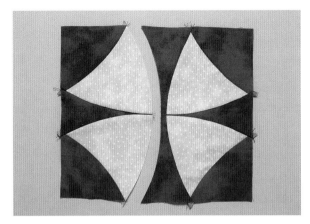

--STEP 2--Only one more seam and we're done! Fold unit 4 back over unit 3. Match the centers at the seamline, not at the edge. You will need to pull back the edge of unit 4 at the center to accurately match the seamlines. Pin with a tiny bite at the center point, placing the pin at the seamline, then pin the following edge.

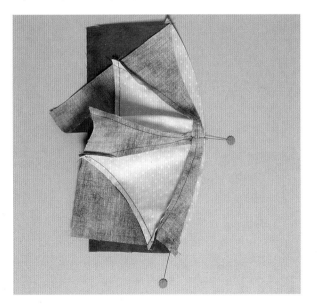

--STEP 3--Sew the seam, keeping the raw edges even and maintaining the $1/4$" seam with your fingers or stiletto. Avoid crossing over or stitching on top of the first long seam, keeping the needle just to the right of that seam. At the center, leave a thread or two between the seams. Don't worry if the $1/4$" seam is off a bit here—it will all work out just fine. Trust me!

--STEP 4--Clip each seam at the side edge $1/4$" in from the outside edge of the block.

--**STEP 5**--Finger press this seam toward unit 3. The Dark long C piece down the middle should be flat.

 BECAUSE OF THE BIAS edges, the blocks will usually be somewhat distorted. Don't trim or square up the outside edges of the blocks. As you sew the blocks and rows together, they will magically square themselves.

--**STEP 6**--Using a dry iron, press the block from the back side first. Remember to keep the skinny part nice and flat. Using a heavy bath towel over your ironing board will prevent the pressed seam from showing through. Now turn over and press the block on the front side.

Congratulations! You've just completed your Winding Ways block. Don't worry if it just doesn't want to press completely flat. Again, because of the many bias seams, there may be some distortion. It's usually not a problem, so don't panic! As the quilt is sandwiched and quilted, the batting and quilting will fill and anchor all of the questionable areas and your finished quilt will look wonderful. Trust me on this one too!

Now that you've mastered the block, you're ready to move on to the quilts!

Welcome to the Projects

WINDING WAYS QUILTS

On the following pages you'll find six quilts using the Winding Ways block. Each takes on a different look, depending on how you use the block. All of the quilts are very simple to do once you've mastered my curved piecing technique. To make it easier to get started, I've given each project a difficulty rating. Although none are truly difficult—some just take a little more time to complete. In fact, my definition of difficult is easy with a couple of twists and bends. These twists and bends might be using more fabrics or making Winding Ways blocks in different sizes, or adding additional simple blocks.

The instructions for each project will tell you what size Winding Ways block I've used to create the quilt. To make your quilt larger or smaller, simply use a larger- or smaller-sized template to make your blocks.

Use the symbols below to choose a project and get started. I hope your first Winding Ways quilt inspires you to try other variations too.

⊕

--EASY EASY--

⊕ ⊕

------EASY------

⊕ ⊕ ⊕

--EASY-WITH-A-TWIST--

Flowers and Dots

Nancy Elliott MacDonald

⊕

This is a basic and simple-to-do Winding Ways quilt, with a pieced border for a finishing touch. It can even be done in a day if you don't have a lot of interruptions! It's a good one to start with because it will get your juices flowing and looking forward to making the next, and the next, and the next . . .

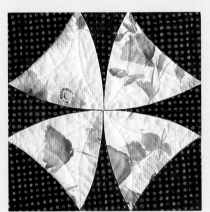

Fabric Requirements

Finished size: 36½" × 36½"

Using 42"-wide cotton fabric and the 9" Winding Ways block

DARK (blocks, border and binding)
  2½ yards

LIGHT (blocks and border)
  2⅓ yards

BACKING
  1¼ yard

SLEEVE
  ¼ yard

BATTING
  41" × 41"

Cutting

Cut the following pieces selvage to selvage.

Dark

▼ For Blocks:

  2 rectangles 22" × 42"

▼ For Border:

  7 strips at 2" wide

▼ For Binding:

  4 strips at 2¼" wide

Light

▼ For Blocks:

  2 rectangles 22" × 42"

▼ For Border:

  8 strips at 2" wide

Making the Blocks

Refer to the Winding Ways—My Way section on page 6 for more information on cutting out and piecing your blocks. Use it as a guide to complete the following steps.

--**Step 1**--Refer to Preparing the Fabric on page 11. Use the Magic Fold technique to fold the 2 Dark rectangles and the 2 Light rectangles, each 22" × the width of the fabric. Use the 9" templates on page 71-73 to cut 5 sets of pieces A, B, and C from both the Light and Dark fabrics.

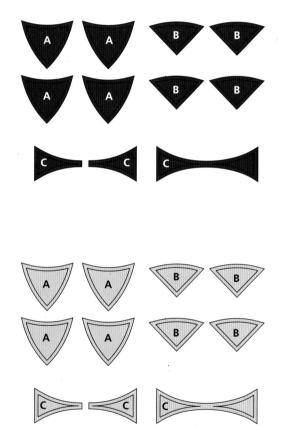

Cut 5 sets from dark and light fabrics.

--**Step 2**--To make Block 1, refer to Making the Winding Ways Block on page 22. Sew together 4 Light A pieces and 4 Dark B and C pieces. Repeat to make a total of 5 of Block 1.

Make 5.

--**Step 3**--To make Block 2, repeat Step 2 above using 4 Dark A pieces and 4 Light B and C pieces. Repeat to make a total of 4 of Block 2 . You will have pieces for 1 Block 2 left over, which can be used for a pillow or the start of another quilt.

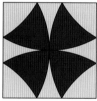

Make 4.

Putting It Together

--**STEP 1**--Alternating Block 1 and Block 2, sew the blocks together into three rows with three blocks in each row as shown. Press the seams open and sew together. Press seams open.

Sew rows together.

--**STEP 2**--To make strip set A for the pieced border, use a $\frac{1}{4}$" seam allowance to sew 1 Light 2" strip between 2 Dark 2" strips. Press the seams toward the dark strips. Repeat to make a total of 2 strip sets.

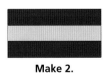

Make 2.

--**STEP 3**--Cut strip set A into 8 segments, each 2" × 5" and 4 segments, each $9\frac{1}{2}$" × 5".

--**STEP 4**--To make strip set B for the pieced border, repeat Step 2, using 2 Light strips and 1 Dark strip. Repeat to make a total of 3 strip sets.

Make 3.

--**STEP 5**--Cut strip set B into 4 segments, each 2" × 5" and 8 segments, each $9\frac{1}{2}$" × 5".

--**STEP 6**--To make Nine-Patch corner blocks, sew together 2 short segments from strip set A and 1 segment from strip set B as shown. Repeat to make a total of 4.

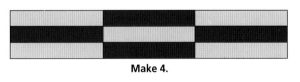

Make 4

--**STEP 7**--Sew together 4 border segments as shown. Press.

Make 4.

--**STEP 8**--Sew 2 border segments to the sides of the quilt. Press.

--**STEP 9**--Sew Nine-Patch corner blocks from Step 6 to each end of the remaining border segments. Sew to the top and bottom of the quilt. Press.

Finishing the Quilt

To finish your quilt, use your favorite techniques or refer to the General Instructions on page 74 to layer and baste the quilt and add quilting and binding. I recommend adding a hanging sleeve and label to your quilt, and you will find more information on these in the General Instructions.

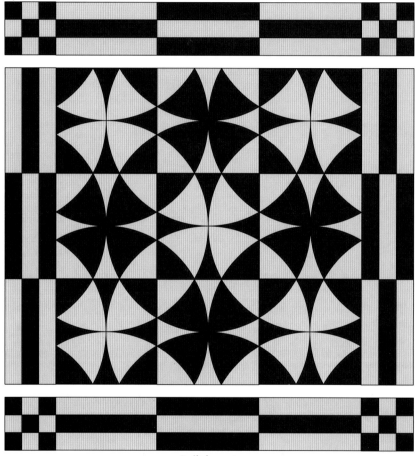

Quilt layout

Another Look

If you prefer, you can add borders to your quilt that are not pieced. Using fresh, spring colors and a soft garden print in the border gives a very different look to the simple, nine-block Winding Ways quilt.

Flower Garden Ways, Nancy Elliott MacDonald

Graphic Medallion

Nancy Elliott MacDonald

EASY

In this quilt there are three different blocks, but it can still prob-ably be done in a day. After I finished the design, I was delighted to see the "bat" shapes surrounding the circle area! What about substituting orange for the dark value, black instead of the medium value and leaving the light value as is. You'll have an instant Halloween quilt!

Fabric Requirements

Finished size: 36½" × 36½"

Using 42"-wide cotton fabric and the 9" Winding Ways block

DARK (blocks, inner border)
1⅛ yards

MEDIUM (blocks, outer border, binding)
1½ yards

LIGHT (blocks)
1 yard

BACKING
1¼ yards

SLEEVE
¼ yard

BATTING
40" × 40"

Cutting

Cut the following pieces, selvage to selvage. *Use the template patterns on pages 71-73. Place templates on strip for cutting this design.*

Dark

▼ For Blocks

Templates A and C   4 strips at 5½"-wide, then use 9" templates to cut 24 A and 4 C pieces

Template B   1 strip at 4½"-wide, then use 9" templates to cut 8 B pieces

▼ For Inner Border

4 strips at 1½"-wide

Medium

▼ For Blocks

Templates A and C   3 strips at 5½"-wide, then use the 9" templates to cut 4 A and 20 C pieces

Template B   1 strip at 4½"-wide, then use the 9" template to cut 4 B pieces

▼ For Outer Border

4 strips at 4"-wide

▼ For Binding

4 strips at 2¼"-wide

Light

▼ For Blocks

Templates A and C   3 strips at 5½"-wide, then use 9" templates to cut 8 A and 12 C pieces

Template B   3 strips at 4½"-wide, then use the 9" template to cut 24 B pieces

Making the Blocks

Refer to the Winding Ways—My Way technique on page 6 for more information on cutting out (using strips) and piecing your blocks. Use it as a guide to complete the following steps.

--**Step 1**--Make 1 of Block 1 using 4 Dark A, 4 Medium B, and 4 Medium C pieces.

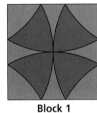

**Block 1
Make 1.**

--**Step 2**--Make 4 of Block 2 using 2 Dark A, 2 Light A, 2 Light B, 2 Dark B, 1 Light C, 1 Dark C, and 2 Medium C pieces in each block.

**Block 2
Make 4.**

--**Step 3**--Make 4 of Block 3 using 3 Dark A, 1 Medium A, 4 Light B, 2 Light C, and 2 Medium C pieces in each block.

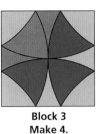

**Block 3
Make 4.**

Putting It Together

--**Step 1**--Arrange the blocks into three rows as shown, rotating Blocks 2 and Blocks 3 to make the design. Sew the blocks together into three rows.

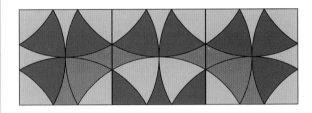

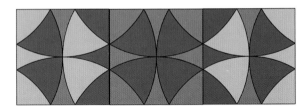

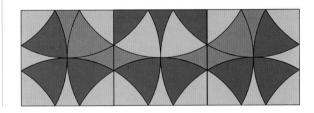

--STEP 2--Sew the rows together.

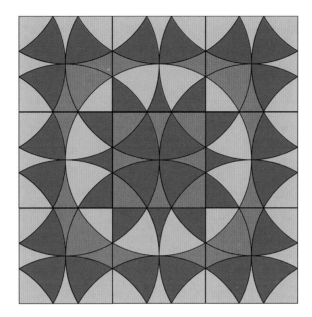

--STEP 3--Refer to Borders on page 74. Using the $1\frac{1}{2}$" dark strips for the inner border and the 4" medium strips for the outer border, add the borders to the quilt.

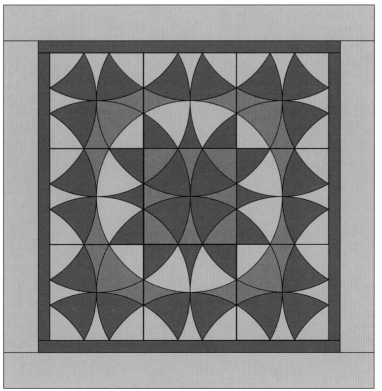

Quilt layout

Finishing the Quilt

To finish your quilt, use your favorite techniques or refer to the General Instructions on page 74 to layer and baste the quilt and add quilting and binding. I recommend adding a hanging sleeve and label to your quilt and you will find more information on these in the General Instructions.

Another Look

Here is *Batty Ways,* the Halloween quilt I described at the beginning of the project. Definitely spooky!

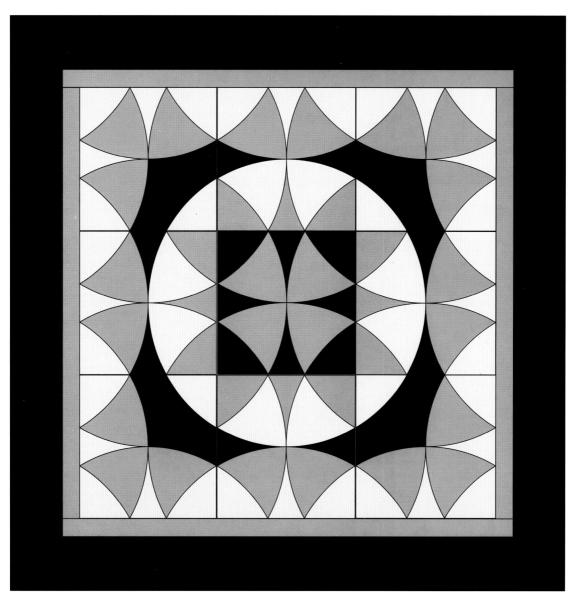

Batty Ways quilt layout

Colorwheel Medallion

Nancy Elliott MacDonald

EASY

In this quilt each block is a different color, but the piecing process is exactly the same. I used four shades of gray and a rainbow set of hand-dyed fabrics in pastel tints, but bright colors would be equally effective. This one will take more than a day—but it will be worth the effort.

Fabric Requirements

Finished size: 25½" × 25½"

Using 42"-wide cotton fabric and the 6" Winding Ways block

DARK GRAY (blocks, binding, inner border)
⅝ yard

MEDIUM GRAY (blocks, outer border)
⅝ yard

LIGHT GRAY (blocks)
⅝ yard

NEARLY WHITE GRAY (blocks)
⅓ yard

8 SOLIDS OR PRINTS (blocks, pieced Zinger border)
Red, orange, yellow, yellow-green, green, blue-green, blue, violet

1 fat quarter or 1 strip, 8" × 22"

BACKING
⅞ yard

HANGING SLEEVE
¼ yard

BATTING
30" × 30"

Cutting

Cut the following selvage to selvage. *Use template patterns on pages 71-73. Place templates on strips for cutting this design.*

Dark Gray
▼ For Binding
3 strips at 2¼"-wide

▼ For Blocks
Template A   1 strip at 4"-wide, then use 6" template to cut 4 A pieces

▼ For Narrow Inner Border
2 strips at ¾"-wide

▼ For Outer Border Corner Squares
From strip remaining for Template A, cut 4 squares, 4" × 4"

Medium Gray
▼ For Outer Unpieced Border
2 strips at 3½"-wide

▼ For Blocks
Template A   2 strips at 4"-wide, then use 6" template to cut 16 A pieces

Light Gray
▼ For Blocks
Template B   2 strips at 3"-wide, then use 6" template to cut 20 B pieces

Template C   1 strip at 3¾"- wide, then use 6" template to cut 12 C pieces

Nearly White Gray
▼ For Blocks
Template A   1 strip at 4"-wide, then use 6"template to cut 8 A pieces

Template B   1 strip at 3"-wide, then use 6" template to cut 4 B pieces

Cutting *continued*

Red
▼ **For Blocks**

Template A, B, C   1 strip at 4"-wide, then use the 6" templates to cut 1 A piece, 2 B pieces, 2 C pieces

▼ **For the Zinger Border**

2 strips at ¾"-wide

Orange
▼ **For Blocks**

Template A, B, C   1 strip at 4"-wide, then use the 6" templates to cut 1 A piece, 1 B piece, 4 C pieces

▼ **For the Zinger Border**

2 strips at ¾"-wide

Yellow
▼ **For Blocks**

Template A, B, C   1 strip at 4"-wide, then use the 6" templates to cut 1 A piece, 2 B pieces, 2 C pieces

▼ **For the Zinger Border**

2 strips at ¾"-wide

Yellow-Green
▼ **For Blocks**

Template A, B, C   1 strip at 4"-wide, then use the 6" templates to cut 1 A piece, 1 B piece, 4 C pieces

▼ **For the Zinger Border**

2 strips at ¾"-wide

Green
▼ **For Blocks**

Template A, B, C   1 strip at 4"-wide, then use the 6" templates to cut 1 A piece, 2 B pieces, 2 C pieces

▼ **For the Zinger Border**

2 strips at ¾"-wide

Blue-Green
▼ **For Blocks**

Template A, B, C   1 strip at 4"-wide, then use the 6" templates to cut 1 A piece, 1 B piece, 4 C pieces

▼ **For the Zinger Border**

2 strips at ¾"-wide

Blue
▼ **For Blocks**

Template A, B, C   1 strip at 4"-wide, then use the 6" templates to cut 1 A piece, 2 B pieces, 2 C pieces

▼ **For the Zinger Border**

2 strips at ¾"-wide

Violet
▼ **For Blocks**

Template A, B, C   1 strip at 4"-wide, then use the 6" templates to cut 1 A piece, 1 B piece, 4 C pieces

▼ **For the Zinger Border**

2 strips at ¾"-wide

IF YOU DON'T WANT to work with ¾" strips to create the Zinger border, cut one 1½" strip of each color, construct one strip set and follow the instructions to create the pieced Zinger border. Adjust narrow inner border and outer border strips accordingly.

Making the Blocks

Refer to the Winding Ways—My Way technique on page 6 for more information on cutting out and piecing your blocks. Use it as a guide to complete the following steps.

--STEP 1--Make nine blocks, each different, following the diagrams below for color placement:

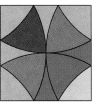
Block 1

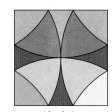
Block 2

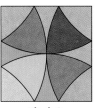
Block 3

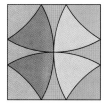
Block 4

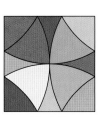
Block 5

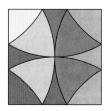
Block 6

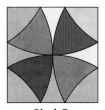
Block 7

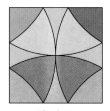
Block 8

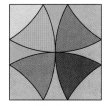
Block 9

Putting It Together

--STEP 1--Arrange the blocks into 3 rows of 3 blocks each and sew the blocks together into rows.

--STEP 2--Sew the rows together.

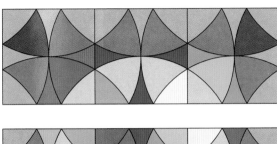

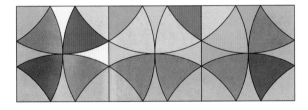

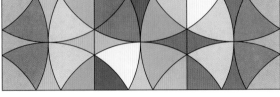

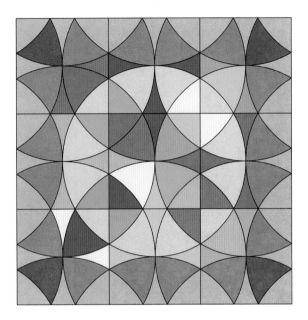

--STEP 3--To make the Zinger border, sew the $3/4$" strips together in the order shown below. Press the seams in one direction. Make two strip sets. The finished strip sets will measure $2^{1}/_{2}$" × 22".

--**Step 4**--Trim off the selvage ends and cut $^3/_4$" segments from the pieced strip set.

--**Step 5**--To create Zinger border, sew 9 segments together, keeping colors in order. Pick out the seam to separate the extra segments from the end and use to begin the next side. Add segments until a little too long for the next side. Pick out the seam to separate the extra segments from the end and continue in this manner until all four sides are constructed.

--**Step 6**--Arrange the Zinger borders so the color order travels around the quilt as shown in the quilt layout below.

--**Step 7**--Sew the dark gray, Zinger and medium gray border strips together as shown in the quilt layout. Sew two sections to the sides of pieced quilt top. Press.

--**Step 8**--Sew a dark gray 4" square to both ends of each border strip. Attach the top and bottom borders.

Finishing the Quilt

To finish your quilt, use your favorite techniques or refer to the General Instructions on page 74 to layer and baste the quilt and add quilting and binding. I recommend adding a hanging sleeve and label to your quilt and you will find more information on these in the General Instructions.

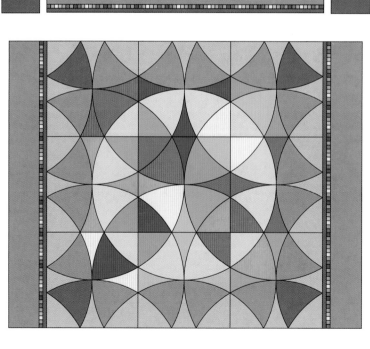

Quilt layout

Amish Stars

Nancy Elliott MacDonald

I've used the Amish color palette of bright, clear colors to create this Winding Ways quilt. Each block is a different color accentuated by the traditional black background. The blocks are of many different colors creating a dramatic pattern on the quilt. Just follow the directions carefully, and you won't have any trouble at all making this eye-catching quilt.

Fabric Requirements

Finished size: 48" × 60"

Using 42"-wide cotton fabric and the 6" Winding Ways Block

DARK (blocks, binding)
  6⅝ yards

18 SOLID COLORS IN THE AMISH COLOR GROUP (blocks)
  ⅛ yard of each color for a total of 2¼ yards

BACKING
  3¾ yards

HANGING SLEEVE
  ½ yard

BATTING
  52" × 64"

Cutting

Cut the following selvage to selvage. *Use the template patterns on pages 71-73. Place templates on strips for cutting this design.*

Dark

▼ **For Blocks**

Template A	25 strips at 4"-wide, then use 6" template to cut 244 A pieces
Template B	14 strips at 3"-wide, then use 6" template to cut 176 B pieces
Template C	20 strips at 3¾"-wide, then use 6" template to cut 284 C pieces

▼ **For Binding**

For bias binding, refer to General Instructions on page 76

240" bias strips cut from a 24" square

AMISH SOLIDS
From each of the 18 different fabrics

▼ **For Blocks**

Template A	1 strip at 4"-wide, then use 6" template to cut 4 A pieces
Template B	Use 4"-wide strip that is already cut, then use 6" template to cut 8 B pieces

TRADITIONAL AMISH QUILTS AVOID the colors with yellow: yellow-green, yellow, yellow-orange, orange, red-orange, and sometimes red—if it's on the orange side. The other colors—reds, violets, blues, and greens (but not yellowish-greens) are fine. I used these 18 colors, but fewer colors may be used, making several blocks from the same color. It would also be perfectly OK for you to use any color you please and to include lots of those with yellow if that's what you prefer.

Making the Blocks

Refer to the Winding Ways—My Way technique on page 6 for more information on cutting out and piecing your blocks. Use it as a guide to complete the following steps. Colors in the examples below will vary from block to block. The examples are only to assist in placement of your colors. See the quilt layout on page 48 to arrange the blocks.

--**Step 1**--Make 18 of Block 1, using 4 colored A, 4 black B, and 4 black C pieces.

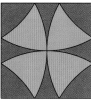

Block 1

--**Step 2**--Make 13 of Block 2, using 4 black A, 2 B of 1 color, 2 B of another color, and 4 black C pieces.

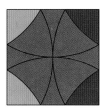

Block 2

--**Step 3**--Make 32 of Block 3, using 4 black A, 2 colored B, 2 black B, and 4 black C pieces.

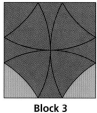

Block 3

Note: Blocks 4, 5, and 6 are partial blocks.

--**Step 4**--Make 14 of Block 4, using 2 black A, 2 colored B, and 1 black C piece.

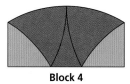

Block 4

--**Step 5**--Make 18 of Block 5, using 2 black A, 2 black B, and 1 black C piece.

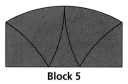

Block 5

--**Step 6**--Make 4 of Block 6, using one black B piece.

Block 6

Putting It Together

--**Step 1**--Refer to the quilt layout to arrange blocks on the floor or design wall. Sew the blocks together into rows, then sew the rows together.

Finishing the Quilt

To finish your quilt, use your favorite techniques or refer to the General Instructions on page 74 to layer and baste the quilt and add quilting and binding. I recommend adding a hanging sleeve and label to your quilt and you will find more information on these in the General Instructions as well.

Quilt layout

Fiesta!

Nancy Elliott MacDonald

This is one of my favorite quilts and that of many of my friends and students. It was inspired by a wonderful piece of woven striped fabric with both warm and cool groups of stripes and a group of brilliantly colored hand-dyed fabrics. They came together perfectly to create *Fiesta!* This one will take a little more time—so have fun with it.

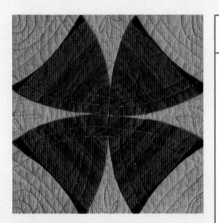

Fabric Requirements

Finished size: 55½"× 55½"

Using 42" wide cotton fabric and the 8½" Winding Ways block

BRILLIANT STRIPES (blocks)
2⅛ yards

INTENSE SOLIDS (blocks)
3⅓ yards

PRINT (blocks, inner and outer borders)
1⅝ yards

BACKING
3⅓ yards

SLEEVE
½ yard

BATTING
60" × 60"

Cutting

Cut the following selvage to selvage. *Use template patterns on pages 71-73. Place templates on strips for cutting this design.*

Brilliant Stripes

▼ For Winding Ways blocks

Template A 14 strips at 5"-wide, then use the 8½" template to cut 100 A pieces

Intense Solids

▼ For Winding Ways blocks

Cut pieces in multiples of 4. Each block requires 4 of each.

Template B 11 strips at 4¼"-wide, then use 8½" template to cut 100 B pieces

Template C 9 strips at 5"-wide, then use 8½" template to cut 100 C pieces

▼ For Nine-Patch Blocks

Template D 15 strips at 1½"-wide, then use template to cut 396 D pieces or a ruler to cut 396 squares, 1½" × 1½"

Print

▼ For Nine-Patch Blocks

Template E 7 strips at 3"-wide, then use template to cut 176 triangles or a ruler to cut 88 squares, 3" × 3", then cut each once diagonally to yield 176 triangles

▼ For Inner Border

6 strips at 1"-wide

▼ For Outer Border

6 strips at 2"-wide

▼ For Binding

6 strips at 2¼"-wide

Making the Blocks

Refer to the Winding Ways—My Way technique Page 6 for more information on cutting out and piecing your blocks. Use it as a guide to complete the following steps. Rearrange the cut pieces into blocks.

--**Step 1**--For Block I, use the A pieces of brilliant stripes and B and C pieces of intense solids to make 25 assorted Block I's, similar to those in the drawing below.

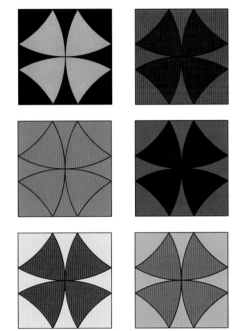

Possible Block 1 variations

--**Step 2**--For Block 2, use the solid squares and the print triangles, to make 44 assorted Nine-Patch blocks similar to those below. Select 5 matching squares of one color and 4 matching squares of another color for each and follow the step-by-step instructions that follow.

Possible Block 2 variations

Putting It Together

--STEP 1--Arrange and sew the blocks in 3 rows of 3 squares each, alternating colors.

--STEP 2--Sew the rows together into Nine-Patch Blocks. Press seams in one direction.

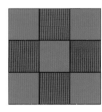

--STEP 3--Add a print triangle to opposite sides of the Nine-Patch block. Press toward the triangles.

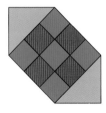

--STEP 4--Add print triangles to the other two sides of the Nine-Patch block. Press toward the triangles.

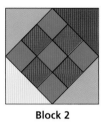

Block 2

--STEP 5--Referring to the quilt layout arrange Block 1 into 5 rows of 5 blocks each. Sew blocks together into rows. Press the seams of the rows in alternating directions. Sew the rows together. Press.

--STEP 6--For the short pieced border, refer to the drawing below and arrange Block 2's into 2 rows of 10 blocks each. Sew blocks together and press seams in one direction. Sew a 1" inner border strip to one side of each row. Press toward the 1" strip.

--STEP 7--For the long pieced border, refer to the drawing below and arrange two more rows of 10 blocks each. Sew blocks together. Add the 1" inner border strip and another Nine-Patch block to each end of both rows. Press seams in one direction. Sew a 1" inner border strip to one side of each pieced border. Press toward the 1" strip.

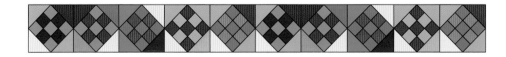

Short pieced border

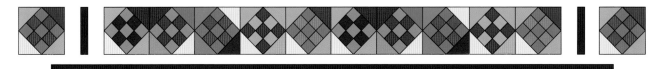

Long pieced border

--STEP 8--Sew the short pieced borders to opposite sides of the quilt top. Press. Sew the longer pieced borders to the other two sides, lining up the narrow inner border strips to match the inner borders.

--STEP 9--Use the 2" strips of print fabric to add the outer border to the quilt.

Finishing the Quilt

To finish your quilt, use your favorite techniques or refer to the General Instructions on page 74 to layer and baste the quilt and add quilting and binding. I recommend adding a hanging sleeve and label to your quilt and you will find more information on these in the General Instructions as well.

Quilt layout

Medallion of Four

Nancy Elliott MacDonald

EASY-WITH-A-TWIST

I love this medallion quilt which came from one of those "what if" thought processes. What if I combined blocks in more than one size in the same quilt? What if I arranged the colors so that there was a circular medallion effect? It naturally followed to work the values to create even more of a medallion effect. Thus, *Medallion of Four* was born.

Fabric Requirements

Finished size: 66" × 66"

Using 42" wide cotton fabric and the 3", 6", 9" and 12" Winding Ways blocks

DARK (blocks, binding)
3½ yards

MEDIUM (blocks)
3 yards

LIGHT (blocks)
5½ yards

BACKING
4 yards

SLEEVE
½ yard

BATTING
70" × 70"

Cutting

Cut the following selvage to selvage. *Use the template patterns on pages 71-73. Place templates on strips for cutting this design.*

Dark

▼ For Blocks

3" block	1 strip at 2½"-wide, then use 3" template to cut 4 A pieces
6" block	9 strips at 3¾"-wide, then use 6" template to cut 88 A pieces
	1 strip at 3"-wide, then use 6" template to cut 8 B pieces
9" block	3 strips at 5"-wide, then use 9" template to cut 16 A pieces
	1 strip at 4¼"-wide, then use 9" template to cut 4 B pieces
12" block	5 strips at 6½"-wide, then use 12" template to cut 24 A pieces
	1 strip at 5¼"-wide, then use 12" template to cut 4 B pieces

▼ For Binding

For bias binding, refer to General Instructions on page 74.
284" of bias strips cut from a 26" square

Medium

▼ For Blocks

3" blocks	1 strip at 2¼"-wide, then use 3" template to cut 12 A pieces
6" blocks	3 strips at 3¾"-wide, then use 6" template to cut 24 A pieces
9" blocks	7 strips at 5"-wide, then use 9" template to cut 32 A pieces
12" blocks	8 strips at 6½"-wide, then use 12" template to cut 40 A pieces

Light

▼ For Blocks

3" blocks	1 strip at 2"-wide, then use 3" template to cut 16 B pieces
	1 strip at 2¼"-wide, then use 3" template to cut 16 C pieces
6" blocks	9 strips at 3"-wide, then use 6" template to cut 108 B pieces
	5 strips at 3¾"-wide, then use 6" template to cut 72 C pieces
9" blocks	5 strips at 4¼"-wide, then use 9" template to cut 44 B pieces
	5 strips at 5"-wide, then use 9" template to cut 48 C pieces
12" blocks	8 strips at 5¼"-wide, then use 12" template to cut 60 B pieces
	8 strips at 6½"-wide, then use 12" template to cut 64 C pieces

Making the Blocks

Refer to the Winding Ways—My Way technique on page 6 for more information on cutting out and piecing your blocks. Use it as a guide to complete the following steps.

Rearrange the cut pieces into blocks.

Block 1

3" blocks—Make 4.

Use 3 Medium A, l Dark A, 4 Light B, and 4 Light C pieces to make each block.

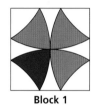

Block 1

Block 2

6" Blocks—Make 4.
9" Blocks—Make 8.
12" Blocks—Make 12.

Use 2 dark A, 2 Medium A, 4 Light B, and 4 Light C pieces to make each block.

Block 2

Block 3

6" Blocks—Make 4.
9" Blocks—Make 4.
12" Blocks—Make 4.

Use 4 Medium A, l Dark B, 3 Light B, and 4 Light C pieces to make each block.

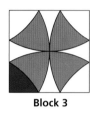

Block 3

Block 4

6" Half Blocks—Make 40.

Use 2 Dark A, 2 Light B, and l Light C piece to make each half block.

Block 4

Block 5

6" Corner Blocks—Make 4.

Use l Dark B piece for each corner block.

Block 5

Putting It Together

--**STEP 1**--Using the photograph and the drawing below as your guide, arrange blocks on design wall or floor. Starting from the center, sew four 3" Block 1's together into 2 rows, and then join rows together with dark corners facing toward the center.

Unit 1

--**STEP 2a**--Sew a 6" Block 2 to 2 sides of unit 1 with Dark A pieces facing center.

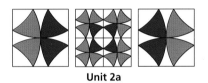

Unit 2a

--**STEP 2b**--Sew together two 6" Block 2's and four 6" Block 3's with Dark patches forming a partial circle and sew to other two sides of unit 2a with the Dark patches facing the center.

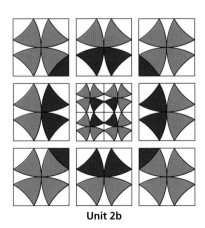

Unit 2b

--**STEP 3a**--Sew together two 9" Block 2's with Dark patches adjoining. Repeat and sew to 2 sides of unit 2b with Dark patches facing the center.

Unit 3a

--**STEP 3b**--Sew together two 9" Block 2's. Sew one 9" Block 3 to each end, Dark patches adjoining. Repeat. Sew to the other 2 sides of unit 3a with Dark patches facing center.

Unit 3b

--**STEP 4a**--Sew together three 12" Block 2's with Dark patches adjoining. Repeat. Sew to two sides of unit 3b.

Unit 4a

--**STEP 4b**--Sew together three 12" Block 2's and sew a 12" Block 3 to each end, Dark patches adjoining. Repeat. Sew these block strips to the other 2 sides of unit 4a with Dark patches facing center.

Unit 4b

--**STEP 5a**--Sew together ten 6" Block 4 half-blocks, Dark patches adjoining. Repeat. Sew to 2 sides of unit 4b with Dark patches facing center.

Unit 5a

--**STEP 5b**--Sew together ten 6" Block 4 half-blocks. Sew a Dark Block 5 quarter-block at each end, Dark patches adjoining. Repeat. Sew to other 2 sides of unit 5a.

Finishing the Quilt

To finish your quilt, use your favorite techniques or refer to the General Instructions on Page 74 to layer and baste the quilt and add quilting and binding. I recommend adding a hanging sleeve and label to your quilt and you will find more information on these in the General Instructions as well.

Quilt layout

Quilting

Quilting is a bit more complicated on this version. I quilted each "round" of the medallion separately. First, the S-curves in-the-ditch. The 3" blocks had in-the-ditch and meandering only. For the other blocks I used a strategy of continuous curves quilting through the colored patches with matching thread. The 6" and 9" blocks had slightly different quilting designs. The 12" blocks combined the quilting design of the 6" and 9" blocks. All of the background areas were quilted with a free-motion meander pattern and white thread. I quilted the medium areas with gold metallic thread because there was gold in the print. In the dark areas I used matching blue thread.

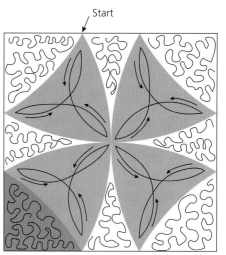

Quilting the 9" blocks

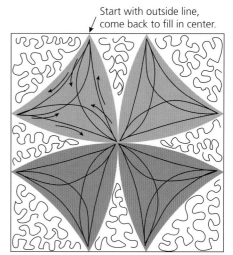

Quilting the 12" blocks

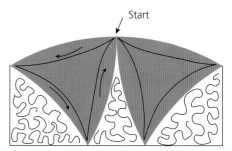

Quilting the 6" outer border half-blocks

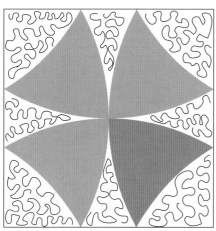

Quilting the 3" blocks

Quilting the 6" blocks

Gallery of Quilts

MORE WINDING WAYS

And there's more . . . the great thing about the Winding Ways block is how many different looking quilts you can create. By changing the fabrics, dark and light values, and the size of the blocks and the quilt, the possibilities are endless. Well, almost endless. If you're like me, once you master the basic block and make your first quilt, you'll be hooked. I'm on number 40 and counting!

For inspiration, here is a selection of more Winding Ways quilts. I have made some of them and others were made by quilting friends who came up with some great ideas of their own. I hope you enjoy looking at them and that they inspire you to come up with your own variations.

Uglies *by Nancy Elliott MacDonald*

80" × 97"

My first Winding Ways blocks were made with fabrics I didn't like—it was only an experiment, after all. The more blocks I made, the better I liked the pattern and the more ugly fabrics I used. This became one of my favorite quilts, but the name *Uglies* stuck.

Kimono Ways *by Nancy Elliott MacDonald*

66" × 81"

Kimono Ways is probably the most complicated Winding Ways quilt I've made. The hand-appliquéd border took about 2 years to complete. The quilt has received a number of prestigious awards at international quilt shows.

Yellow and Blue *by Nancy Elliott MacDonald*

86" × 93"

I just had to include this quilt because it is so eye-catching. It was among the finalists nominated for the "100 Best Quilts of the Century" exhibit sponsored by the International Quilt Association in 2000, and has traveled to Europe to be exhibited. The 87 prints were either yellow or blue.

Purples Galore *by Nancy Elliott MacDonald*

42" × 54"

Purples Galore demonstrates how dramatic a monochromatic color scheme can be. Note that in the outer row of blocks every other block is an unpieced fabric square.

Black and White *by Nancy Elliott MacDonald*

72" × 88"

This is another monochromatic/neutral quilt including more than 100 different black-and-white prints. The blocks were pieced in 1997, the quilt was assembled in 2002, and quilted and finished in 2003.

Flower Power Ways *by Nancy Elliott MacDonald*

35½" × 35½"

Here's an example of my class project quilt which uses nine blocks with simple, unpieced Zinger and outer borders. I've seen a number of my students complete the top during a one-day class.

Winding Ways Through the USA *by Helen Shaw Powell*

75" × 84"

Helen's quilt used many pieces from her extensive Batik collection and was hand pieced in the car during an extended trip around the country, hence the name. This is a wonderful, splashy, feeling-really-good kind of a quilt.

A Bride's Quilt for Bridget *by Nancy Arseneault*

63" × 81"

A Bride's Quilt for Bridget was made for a lucky new daughter-in-law. Nancy's super scrappy approach used a different print for each patch in the block. This is a monochromatic approach I want to try, working my way around the color wheel.

Don't It Make You Want to Sing *by Judi Dains*

Award-winning wearable artist Judi Dains works with tiny 3" and 4" Winding Ways blocks to create some of her amazing garments. Judy told me that when she saw my quilt *Fiesta!* (page 49) at our local quilt show, she overheard someone say, "It just makes me want to sing." That's what she named her jacket that was inspired by that quilt.

**Winding Ways
Template Pattern B & C
For 3", 6", 9", 12" Blocks**

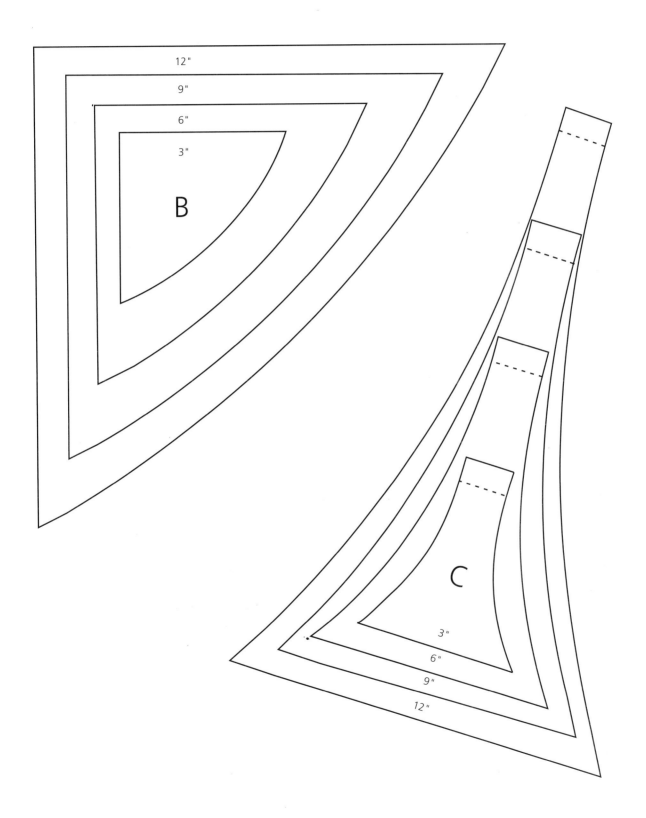

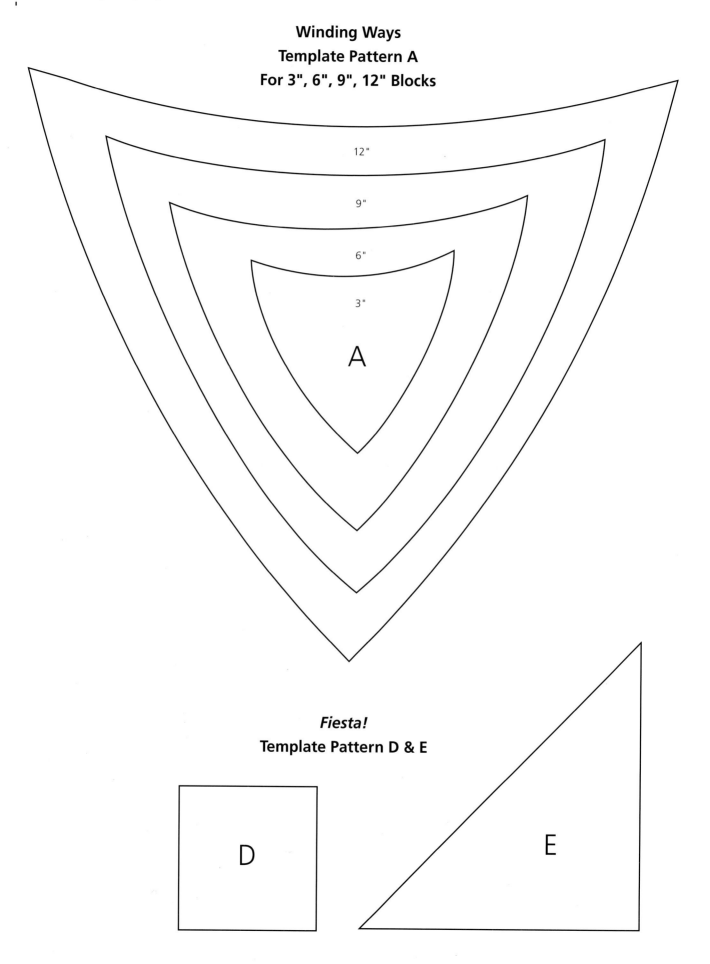

**Winding Ways
Template Pattern A
For 3", 6", 9", 12" Blocks**

12"

9"

6"

3"

A

Fiesta!
Template Pattern D & E

D

E

Winding Ways
Template Pattern A, B, C
For 8½" Block

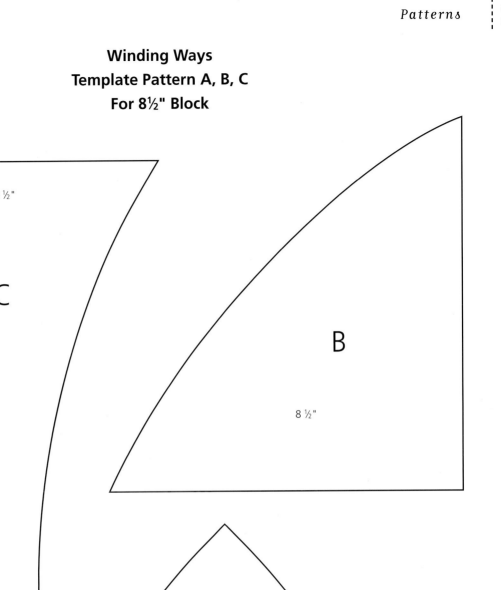
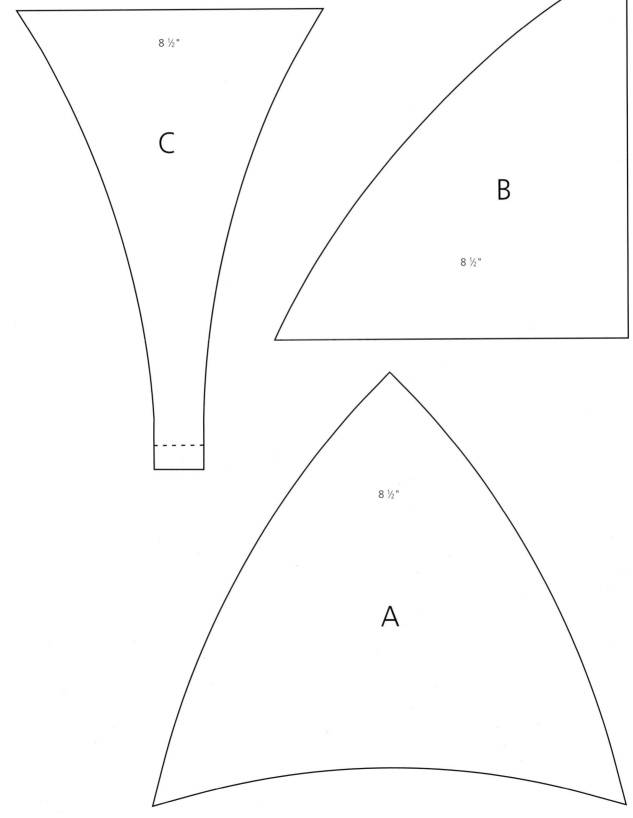

8 ½ "

C

B

8 ½ "

8 ½ "

A

General Instructions

There are a number of different finishing techniques that will work to complete your quilt. You may have your own favorite methods, which work fine for you, but I'll give you information here on the finishing techniques that work the best for me.

Borders

--**STEP 1**--Measure the quilt from top to bottom through the center. Piece strips if necessary and trim to measured length to make the two side borders. Sew to the quilt and press toward the borders.

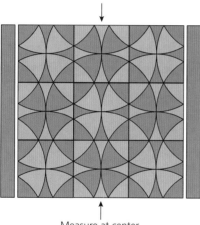

Measure at center.

--**STEP 2**--Measure the quilt from side to side including the side borders through the center. Piece strips if necessary and trim to the measured length to make top and bottom borders. Sew to top and bottom and press toward the borders. To add multiple borders, repeat the above steps for each border.

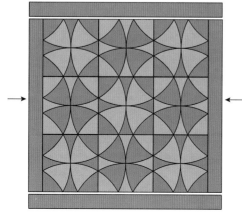

Measure at center.

Pressing

Place a large bath towel over the ironing board to prevent the seam allowance lines from showing through to the quilt top after pressing. Carefully press the whole quilt top, paying attention to straightening seam lines. I like to use sizing and a dry iron. Spray lightly and evenly. Wait a few seconds, pat down with fingers if needed, then press gently until dry.

I prefer sizing to spray starch because starch leaves more of a coating on the fabric whereas sizing penetrates and relaxes the fibers, adding body and allowing you to smooth, straighten, and flatten a badly distorted block or quilt. Be sure your top is pressed flat and wrinkle free.

Preparing the Quilt Back

Backing fabric requirements for each project are shown in each materials list. When choosing backing fabric, consider whether it will shadow through to show on the front side. This is usually not a problem if you use cotton or mostly-cotton batting. Quilt backs should be pressed carefully before layering the quilt.

Sandwiching the Quilt

Sandwiching is the process by which the three layers, backing, batting, and quilt top, are joined together temporarily so that they can be quilted. My students say I'm really obsessive about preparing the sandwich. That's true—but my quilts don't get pleats on the back, and I'm able to manage awkward areas on the top layer by paying careful attention to how I put it together.

--**STEP 1**--Begin by spreading the backing wrong side up and securing it. You can tape the edges with masking tape or use clips if you're working on a table or T-pins if you're working on the carpet.

--**STEP 2**--Center the batting on top, smoothing out any folds. Place the quilt top right side up on top of the batting and backing, making sure it's centered. Again, carefully smooth out any wrinkles by patting from the center outward toward the edges.

--**STEP 3**--Baste the quilt layers together with safety pins placed a minimum of 3"–4" apart, again beginning in the center and moving toward the edges. I think safety pins work better than hand basting if you plan to machine quilt your project.

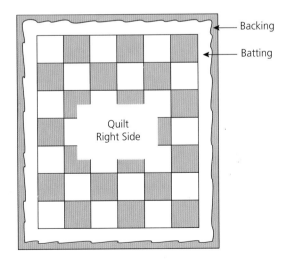

Backing

Batting

Quilt Right Side

MAKE SURE IT'S STRAIGHT To make sure your lines are straight and the quilt is square, bend or lie down to look at it with your eyes at "quilt level." Any wobbly lines will jump out at you. Gently shift the top to straighten. Careful pinning will keep them straight.

--**STEP 4**--When I finish pinning, I use straight pins to anchor the quit and hand baste ¼" around the outside edge of the quilt top, using quilting thread and long stitches. This extra step goes a long way in helping to stabilize the outside edge of the quilt.

--**STEP 5**--Trim the batting to about 1" beyond the edge of the quilt top. Many quilters serge or zigzag around the edge, but my experience has been that this tends to stretch the outside edge.

--**STEP 6**--After removing the tape, pins, or clips that were anchoring the quilt backing to the table or other flat surface, I fold the backing over the edge of the quilt top and pin it about ¼" from the edge with about 3" between the pins. Or, if I have time, I even hand baste this step. These extra steps stabilize the edge of the quilt while it is being handled during the quilting process. It also protects the edges of the fabrics and batting, keeping them together. For me it is worth the extra effort.

SOME QUILTERS ARE HAVING good results using spray adhesive to baste their quilts. Although the manufacturers assure us that they are safe and will wash out, I don't use them because they don't allow me to manipulate the layers as I machine quilt.

Quilting

I am a machine quilter and enjoy quilting many of my quilts myself. I've included some tips and ideas on how I go about machine quilting a Winding Ways quilt.

First, I quilt in-the-ditch on the outside edge of the pieced portion of the quilt. This stabilizes the borders. I might also quilt in-the-ditch along the seams between blocks and rows, which is probably a good idea on your first Winding Ways quilt.

Next, quilt in-the-ditch in an S-Curve line beginning at any point on the edge of the pieced area and continuing until all curved seams are quilted. The 9" blocks often need more quilting, so I may add another line of S-curves going into the pieces. Occasionally I also quilt free-motion motifs within the block.

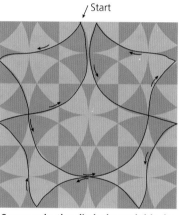

S-curves in-the-ditch through blocks

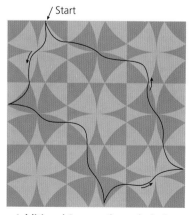

Additional S-curve through design

If you didn't stitch in-the-ditch between the blocks, the area where four block corners meet will often puff up and need quilting to hold it in place. Another place often needing a little extra quilting is at the middle sides of the blocks. One option is to use free-motion techniques to quilt motifs in the corner and side areas as well as in the block pieces themselves.

Bias Strips

Bias strips are cut on the diagonal line of the fabric. They are used in binding to go around curves without wrinkling or puckering.

--**Step 1**--Fold down the corner of a straight piece of fabric, forming a triangle. Cut on this folded line, which is the bias of fabric.

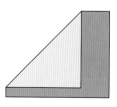

--**Step 2**--Using a see-through ruler and rotary cutter, measure from the bias edge and cut strips the width you need.

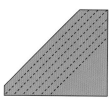

Binding

I always get the binding cut and ready to go before I start quilting. Otherwise, I've found it might be days or weeks before I get it put onto the quilt! I cut my bindings 2$\frac{1}{4}$"-wide, but you may prefer yours narrower or larger.

--**STEP 1**--Piece together the binding strips using a diagonal seam to make a continuous binding strip. Press the seams open, then press the entire strip in half lengthwise with wrong sides together. I like to use a little spray sizing here when I prepare the folded binding strips.

--**STEP 2**--Remove the pinning or basting to release the backing that was folded up over the top edge, but don't remove the basting line along the quilt edge.

--**STEP 3**--Unfold the backing and batting and smooth it out beyond the edge of the top. If the edges are uneven, mark new, straight corner and outer edge lines with chalk or other easily removable pencil or other marker. I prefer using chalk.

--**STEP 4**--With raw edges even, pin the binding to the edge of the quilt starting a few inches away from the corner, and leave the first few inches of the binding unattached. Start sewing using a $\frac{1}{4}$" seam allowance.

--**STEP 5**--Stop $\frac{1}{4}$" away from the first corner, backstitch one stitch, and pivot the quilt with the needle down.

--**STEP 6**--Lift the needle and fold the binding at a right angle so it extends straight above the quilt.

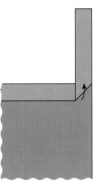

--**STEP 7**--Bring the binding down even with the edge of the quilt.

--**STEP 8**--Begin sewing at the folded edge and continue in this manner until the binding is sewn to the quilt top.

--**STEP 9**--Finish the binding by folding the beginning end $\frac{1}{4}$" and overlapping it with the ending end, trimming off any leftover binding.

--**STEP 10**--Trim the excess batting and backing, leaving about $\frac{1}{4}$" of batting extending beyond the quilt top edge. This leaves enough extra to stuff the binding nicely after it is turned and sewn.

--**STEP 11**--Fold the binding to the back of the quilt and hand stitch in place.

Adding A Hanging Sleeve

If you know your quilt will never hang on a wall or in a quilt show, you may skip this step, but I automatically attach a hanging sleeve after I hand sew the binding to the back of the quilt. That way, I have a sleeve that matches, or at least coordinates, with the back just in case I need it.

Cut a strip of fabric $8\frac{1}{2}$" by the width of your quilt minus $1\frac{1}{2}$". Turn each short end under $\frac{1}{4}$" twice and machine stitch. Sew the long edges together with a $\frac{1}{4}$" seam. Press the seam open.

Center the sleeve at the top of the quilt back with seam toward the quilt and one fold barely touching the sewn edge of the binding. Hand stitch the top and bottom long edges and the under layer of the ends, making sure the top layer is open to accommodate a hanging rod.

Making the Labels

I'm sure you noticed that I said "labels" . . . not "label." Yes, I put at least two labels on every quilt I finish. One of the labels includes washing instructions. When I add this I know I've done everything I can to make sure the quilt is washed carefully. On the label, I instruct the owner to wash in the washing machine in warm water with a gentle detergent, agitating manually. Then rinse, again agitating manually. Spin, remove the quilt, and dry flat. When it is barely damp, fluff in the dryer for a few minutes to soften the batting and fabrics.

This care label is especially good for people who have never owned a quilt. I'm just looking out for the quilt's comfort and safety!

The second label includes the name, date, size, and other important information about the quilt. This might include who it was made for and the occasion it celebrates, whether it was an original design, fiber content, etc.

I print my labels using my computer and laser printer. I iron freezer paper to muslin and feed them through the printer manually. I let the printed fabric dry for 24 hours, then carefully peel off the freezer paper. Next, I heat set with a hot iron for about 2 minutes.

I wash the quilt before I add the labels. It's only when the quilt has been labeled and washed that I consider it really finished.

Keeping a Record of your Quilt

For every quilt I make, I keep a 3" × 5" index card that includes any information that I might wish I could remember later! I start it when I begin the quilt and include the same information that I put on the label, plus anything else that I think might be important, such as how long it took me to do the machine quilting. Whenever possible, I attach a photograph of the quilt to the card. They go into a box next to my sewing machine and are stored by the year they were made. I also keep other records in the computer, but if I get behind on my computer records, this way I always find the information I need.

About the Author

Nancy started quilting in 1988 at age 50, inspired by her "quilt-less" first grandson, but this certainly wasn't her first experience with sewing. She was only eight years old when she started sewing on her mother's old White sewing machine.

She grew up hearing, "We can make that," so that was what she learned to do. She made clothing, dolls, tailored woolen garments, wedding dresses, draperies, slipcovers, and upholstery, but that was only the beginning. For her sons she made ski pants and parkas, sleeping bags, backpacks, and even tents.

She began teaching quilting in 1995, specializing in curved-seam piecing by machine, which today remains her teaching focus. She also creates commission and art quilts and has won many awards at local, national, and international quilt exhibitions. Her work has also been published in a number of quilting periodicals.

Active in her local quilt guild, she also mentors beginning quilt artists. Her favorite activity is simply making quilts and she looks forward to having more time to do so. She and her husband Mac share their home in Carmichael, California, with lots of quilts and lots and lots of fabric.

Resources

WINDING WAYS TEMPLATES are available from the author.
For ordering information on these, and other curved templates she
has designed, call 1 (916) 966-5317 or email her at nancymac@nancymac.com
Visit her website at www.nancymac.com

Index

Other Fine Books from C&T Publishing

15 Two-Block Quilts: Unlock the Secrets of Secondary Patterns, Claudia Olson

America from the Heart: Quilters Remember September 11, 2001, Karey Bresenhan

Bouquet of Quilts, A: Garden-Inspired Projects for the Home, Edited by Jennifer Rounds & Cyndy Lyle Rymer

Celebrate the Tradition with C&T Publishing: Over 70 Fabulous New Blocks, Tips & Stories from Quilting's Best, C&T Staff, Edited by Liz Aneloski and Joyce Lytle

Contemporary Classics in Plaids & Stripes: 9 Projects from Piece O' Cake Designs, Linda Jenkins & Becky Goldsmith

Crazy with Cotton: Piecing Together Memories & Themes, Diana Leone

Cut-Loose Quilts: Stack, Slice, Switch, and Sew, Jan Mullen

Dresden Flower Garden: A New Twist on Two Quilt Classics, Blanche Young

Fantastic Fans: Exquisite Quilts & Other Projects, Alice Dunsdon

Flowering Favorites from Piece O' Cake Designs, Becky Goldsmith & Linda Jenkins

Hidden Block Quilts: • Discover New Blocks Inside Traditional Favorites • 13 Quilt Settings • Instructions for 76 Blocks, Lerlene Nevaril

Make Any Block Any Size: Easy Drawing Method, Unlimited Pattern Possibilities, Sensational Quilt Designs, Joen Wolfrom

Mariner's Compass Quilts: New Directions, Judy Mathieson

New Look at Log Cabin Quilts, A: Design a Scene Block-by-Block PLUS 10 Easy-to-Follow Projects, Flavin Glover

Patchwork Persuasion: Fascinating Quilts from Traditional Designs, Joen Wolfrom

Reverse Appliqué with No Brakez, Jan Mullen

Shoreline Quilts: 15 Glorious Get-Away Projects, compiled by Cyndy Rymer

Simply Stars: Quilts That Sparkle, Alex Anderson

Totally Tubular Quilts: A New Strip-Piecing Technique, Rita Hutchens

Tradition with a Twist: Variations on Your Favorite Quilts, Blanche Young & Dalene Young-Stone

When Quilters Gather: 20 Patterns of Piecers at Play, Ruth B. McDowell

Workshop with Velda Newman, A: Adding Dimension to Your Quilts, Velda E. Newman

FOR MORE INFORMATION, ASK FOR A FREE CATALOG:

C&T Publishing, Inc.
P.O. Box 1456
Lafayette, CA 94549
(800) 284-1114
Email: ctinfo@ctpub.com
Website: www.ctpub.com

FOR QUILTING SUPPLIES:

Cotton Patch Mail Order
3405 Hall Lane, Dept. CTB
Lafayette, CA 94549
(800) 835-4418
(925) 283-7883
Email: quiltusa@yahoo.com
Website: www.quiltusa.com